The Arc of Love

by

Anthony Signorelli

Walden Woods Press

ISBN: 979-8-9953406-0-7

Walden Woods Press
12255 Holly Lake Road
Drummond, WI 54832

Contents

Blackbirds at Dawn

In an apartment in St. Paul,
a man stands in the window,
looking east. Red rays
and dawn's rosy fingers
spread across a sky
whose message is nothing
...but possibility.

Black birds swirl in unison
as if the undulating air
were two lovers on which
they rode; up and down,
on and off... One can only see
the pure joy of instinct
as the birds obey an unseen
force—the one
that makes even God blush.

That man soothes his heart
in the knowledge the blackbirds
confer. Their story signals
something we cannot know.
There isn't an idea that can
cause that experience; only
the inexplicable joy of the divine
instinct when the right man
and the right woman join.

Presence is everything.
Longing is something.
Absence, a sin to endure.
And here he is, standing alone.

The sun rises and says all these
things, yet he stands alone.
He thanks the sun. He thanks
the blackbirds. He dreams
of her with the saddest
joy-filled heart on Earth.

Accepting Your Love

Peewee bird calls in the pine woods.
A distant jay caws.
Squirrel chatters overhead
as if to scold an impetuous child.
I sit in the silent, still air.
Freshness fills my nostrils
as joy for you pervades everything.

As the critters live their lives this morning,
you are present—your shining smile,
the beaming light within you,
the intensity of your love for me.
I have never been loved this way.
Your heart must channel it from the Earth.
Your being mixes the power of the moon.
You make no comparisons; we do not compete.
You have no need for me; only continuing desire.

I am gifted with your love
as it settles in this still air,
as it reaches me on the song of birds.
I am open. I accept the gift you offer.
I cherish that gift for all that it is.
And as I do, the sun smiles,
the moon nods her enduring approval;
Squirrel, jay, and the peewee bird
sound out their view that now
everything is right with the world.

Our Sacred Temple

What would happen if I call to you
across this great valley? What if
my smoke signals rose beautifully—
would you see my heart?
Could you see in the smoke
of my fire, a phallus,
the male god in me
seeking to love the goddess in you?

And if you could, would you
meet me in that fertile valley?
Let me join you
in the deepest place known to man?

We would find God in that valley.
As he connects to mother Earth,
so we connect to each other—
in bodily spirit and divine joy.

Here's the deal: I'm calling you.
That smoke is there. The god
and the goddess are ready.
Come here. Let's go together
...and enter the temple prepared for us.

Love Stone

This morning I wake
and extend my arm
to where you would be,
but aren't, today.
My heart sinks,
a stone drifting
down through the water
to the bottom of the lake.
That's a cold, lonely place —
no place for a heart,
really, but there I am.

And then the smile comes...
I remember our lips touching,
and the smile grows;
our dance, your hand in mine,
and the smile grows.
Snuggling away the hot night,
my lips part, the smile widens,
this smile is taking up my face!

This must be what
one needs to get a stone
up from the bottom of a lake.
Shh! It's a secret!
And I intend to tell
the whole world!

The Sweetness of You

How could I not be happy?
Today you come toward me,
zipping along over the miles,
a hummingbird returning
from another home, to my side
where you belong.
My heart bursts at the thought.

Your picture melts something inside,
and although they don't say it,
sailors who see me ask:
What's up with him?
The answer is: I have a secret.
It makes me smile.
The honey in my heart
is the divine sweetness of you.

Lake Love

You sleep downstairs
the edge of the lake lapping small waves
to the edge of your dream.
It could be me, licking your heart,
caressing the breast of your being.
I watch those waters ripple.

All the way from two stories up,
I feel your hands softly holding my heart.
This is how it has been for us.
Today, it's a cool breeze.
No eagle. No hawk.

Our hearts sail over the water
as if they'd known forever
that this day would come.
There is blue sky and there are white birds.
And I hear the constant drumming
of the one heart that loves me.

Morning Glory

With you upstairs,
your curves sliding out of your robe,
I stand in morning glory,
my hands on your waist
and we kiss.
The stars spin away.
The sun veers off and sets in the north.
The world could fall apart
and I would not know and would not care.
...because of you.
It's your gorgeous joy,
the sparkle in your eye,
that infectious smile.
We kiss—oh, do we kiss—
this morning's glory
disappears into the depths of you
where together, we touch
the divine god within us all.

Four Swans and You

When four swans swept the south shore,
Satan saddled back into his hole
so love could flourish, its sound
singing and ringing over the water,
stillness soothing its own slow way.

I saw those swans and thought of you;
the white smile belying all I must know —
the shine inside, the light beaming,
one life to another, as if to guide
both lives to each other's side.
It is like this with you; we belong together.

Lovers may be in each other all along,
but the joy bursts into life only
when we find each other, and join,
saying, "Hello Love! Come. Sit down..."

So we sit together, hand in hand,
eye to eye, heart to heart. We pray
to the divinity we each know,
honor the God in the other, and sing
our lives open, four swans sweeping our love.

Mystery of Our Love

—for Cheryl on Valentine's Day, 2021

After raining all night,
a mist hangs over the lake,
the shoreline grey and undefined,
the sky just beginning to lighten.

When a man and woman love each other,
days can be shrouded in this mystery.
Clear edges are not needed,
light is best only for seeing the other's eyes.

And so this morning I turn to you,
caress your soft breast, and prepare
my hardness to enter you
in the softest place God ever made.

The loon's cry rises from that thick mystery.
We are carried on that sound.
We are pushed into distant bays
and the wild corners of this great lake
that is our love. Being human,
we swim or paddle across the surface.
We see the glorious sky as the sun rises,
we are held up by the mysterious forces below,
and the warm moistness of our togetherness
pronounces, "We are here! We are here!"
And so we are.

Now, the loon's call has gone quiet.
The mist is lifting. The shoreline trees
can be seen against the sky.
Our love shines through our bodies,
And rides on the first rays of sunlight.
The mystery of our love revealed.

Some Lines on Snow and Love

Snow falls to cover the tracks,
hides everywhere I've been.
No one will know; perhaps not care.
First the mouse tracks, then the squirrel.
Fox prints disappear, then coyote.
Deer are last, the wolf does not move.
There are no bear tracks—they're all sleeping.

Through this whiteness
I long for you. So many miles
between us. Something is right
and something is not right
about this distance;
either way, it leaves me groping
in the dark, reaching for you.
Each time my arms come up empty.

Is this how love works?
I'm not sure. My declarations
do not matter. Only this feeling
inside, this longing, this missing—
these are the universal experiences
we all know. And in my mind's eye,
your beautiful face comes
through the snow, the gift of an angel,
and my heart pours out the window.

The snow keeps adding to the whiteness.

There are no tracks anywhere—
only those many empty miles.
I trudge silently toward
where I saw that angel,
the gift of your face again.
I can't wait for the snow to stop,
the car to run, and for me
to fly back to you.

A Healing Poem

The woman of my dreams has moved into
a silent orbit, traversing past
my place, to and from work,
I imagine, with her pain riding
alongside—orbiting me and my pain—
so here we go missing each other
and confronting our lost ideals.

There is no telling how love manifests;
doors open and you have to walk through.
Holes open and you simply fall in...
or you orbit, circling around the gravity
of the other person's heart—
suspended in hope and disbelief
as bad images fill the empty void.

Real love resides in the ability to heal.
Patience, the fertilizer of love, holds us;
we do well to slow down, consider...
Those bad images are fear speaking.
It is the work of lovers to confront fear,
to demand evidence, to believe only
what is real; we must not succumb
to the fear that would otherwise destroy.

You are not what I fear; I am not
what you fear. We are the tangible participants
in a love dance; the healing is in the steps

we take, the rhythm of the music,
your hand in mine. Each step is a new world
where fear dissipates and love flourishes.

A Broken Heart in Sand

There are times when starlight
goes missing from the sky,
the beaver returns to its den alone,
or a heart perseveres, one part torn off.

It is like this today as you fly off
to important missions in the world.
Does anyone know what they carry
on these trips? What they leave behind?

I cannot know what goes in your bag,
nor the brilliance your soul will shine forth;
I lie here in the sand, wondering...
a broken clam shell discarded by the hungry animal.

Some truth needs to be said,
but I don't know what it is.
The root of my being is reeds in the lake bottom;
from here I shall not be moved.

Oh... The starlight, the beaver, and that
broken heart? They will find their place.
My feet remain in the lake bottom,
standing here, waiting for you.

The Morning After a Misunderstanding

Today, I woke with that soft feeling,
the attraction to you that opens a new world.
Your skin, your eyes, your smile—they glow
out at me, shining into the world,
and say, I'm here! I love you! I want you!

I have never been loved this way.
Yours is an undefended heart,
open to me in joy, happy to greet me,
pleased, it seems, that I am present in your life.
Some men know this love. Until you, I never did.

And so the smooth swaying of summer
passes by our whispering lips;
it comes in kisses, and rarely misses the chance
to blossom fully into the love we share.
You, my love, are the woman of my dreams.

That soft joy and openness calls out the same
from me; I am invited fully into your deep heart.
I like it here. I am glad to answer the call.
For my love is an everlasting fountain,
whose waters originate in God's green home.

You and I will hold this dance. Our stance
is open, inviting. Something in each of us—
very mysterious—merges with the other.
We give. We receive. We come together.
And the love of our joy-filled lives goes on forever.

Robin's Song

I sit here trying to work
while my body weeps for you.
Somewhere, a robin sings,
calling its mate to its own treetop.
That bird is me,
and this is my song.

The love in my heart will not stop;
not even I, by an act of will,
can make it stop. Like the instinctual bird,
I must sing, I must love.
It is the instinct God gave—
to find the mate to whom you belong;
when you do, that love will not end.
And I found that mate in you.

Even with the robin, there are complications.
The materials needed to build
are not available;
A hawk attacks the nest.
Does that mean the robin, in love, stops singing?
No! The robin sings all the louder
with what God gave him.
He praises his love,
calls to his lady,
as I call to you.

What we have is instinctual and rare.

In desperation and agony, I—yes, I—
this flawed and imperfect bird—
nearly destroyed it.
But one cannot destroy the sacred.
Life happens within and among it.
Pain comes, and then joy.
I accept both, and I choose joy.

In the twilight of the day,
the wind dies down.
The forest quiets.
Just down the shoreline,
I hear it—the robin sings!
Its voice is happy and satisfied,
as if it knew all along
the final place at which we would arrive.
The nest is right. The two are happy together.
God's instincts are satisfied.
And as the moon rose,
I swear I saw it smile.
This will be ours. And I love you.

Pure Sweetness That Night

Today is the anniversary of
the first time we kissed.
I will never forget that night.
Our conversation over sushi,
the way you threw your arms
around my neck at the back of the bar
and danced like there was no tomorrow.
The snuggle on that park bench
and the first moment our lips touched.

Pure sweetness that night.

My body knew. As we kissed,
the city began to swirl.
Nothing else mattered.
I was sure of something divine
happening—and I was right.
We walked to the river overlook,
and there we kissed again.
We both felt old pains drain away,
giving them to the Mississippi
to carry to the sea.
We walked, stopped, kissed again.
We peered into each other's eyes.
We saw a soul that matched ours,
met us right where we needed to be.

Pure sweetness that night.

You ignited a flame that night,
an inextinguishable flame.
We both knew: Here is the chemistry,
here is the flame, here is
the partner to my soul.
And we were not wrong.
That fire has burned in me
ever since. Yes, there are problems.
Clearly, I made mistakes.
But that flame? It is
what brought us here tonight.
It has burned through it all.
My fire for you will not rest.

Pure sweetness that night.

And so, here we are again.
Overlooking a great river,
holding pain we may offer to it,
pain that it can carry
once again, all the way to the sea.
Please come here. Let me hold you.
Let's take our pain
and give it to the water.
Let's pour it out,
and let the river take it away.

As the pain drains away,
I'll still hold you.
I am sorry I caused so much pain.

Let's watch it go
and give it the respect it deserves.
As it goes, may our hearts open
so love may pour in again.

Pure sweetness *this* night.

I can't explain it really,
but I am a transformed man.
Through the pain, my love has deepened.
If you will have me,
I will kiss you again.
Right here. Right now.
I'll lose myself in the touch of your lips.
And joy will ride its wild horse
down to the center of my heart.

And if you won't kiss me yet,
I will wait. For this love
endures and will endure—
inextinguishable is the flame.
But make no mistake.
I want to kiss you now.
I want you to feel my heat.
I want you to know
how the flame burns for you.

Pure sweetness this night.

Land

Do you feel the ground
back under your feet?
Our love, that *stormy sea
of moving emotion,*
returned me here to stand,
or sit, on my land.
The water is salty
like tears; the wind
painful, loaded with fears.
I did not ask for
calm seas or solid ground,
but here I am,
my love being carried off—
away from me,
away from you—
the two places
it could actually be.
My feet are on dry land.
The salty tears sting
the wound; the wind
lifts the eagle who
soars silently overhead.

The Woman on a White Horse

Once I saw a white horse
bounding down the hillside.
It carried a woman
who came too close,
swept me off my feet.
In joy I arched my back,
In thrill I flew with her
as the horse ascended
into the air, the clouds, the sky.

Ah, but horses don't really fly
and despite the thrill
I was trapped.
I had no horse.
I could not fly.
There was no way down.

And so, I ignored the ground.
I hung on for the joy.
The woman and I
made love in the clouds
and I soon dreamed
there was nothing in this world
but clouds.
I suggested we marry on one
and she said yes.
She insisted on bringing the horse.

That should have been a sign.
But I discovered a funny thing:
You can't build a house on a cloud.
She wanted to try.
I thought earth was a better idea.
But with her on earth,
the thrill was gone.
The joy left us.
We wanted to believe
that it was our horse;
that we flew though we cannot;
that a fairyland can be forever...
all that fell away.
I looked at her
and I did not like what I saw.

After a good fight
she'd disappear
and later ride by on that white horse.
Sometimes I got on it.
Other times I waved in appreciation.
It was, after all, a beautiful horse.
Today, I see the trap—
It is a horse of her world, not mine.
It is a horse of adoration, not love.
And it carried no feeling anymore.

And so when she comes by now,
I wave.
I wave with no longing,

no want, no desire.
I do not wave to her to beckon,
I wave her on.
I wave to bless her journey.
I wave to watch her pass.
Her white shirt blows
as I watch her back
and her white horse
disappear into the forest.
I imagine they will head
back up that hill
and go over the top.
And as they go, I doubt
I will ever see them again.

Love's Silhouette

She stands there at the door waiting,
the one I love so much,
her hair a silhouette
against the light from inside.
She's waiting. She won't come out.
I step a little closer
and can see her shining face
and her brilliant eyes
in the shadow of the light.
I think again—what have I done?
I open my arms toward her
but she does not come.
She does not move.
My heart swells and tears rise,
my face puffy with the sadness inside.
For to go to her, I lose me.
Or do I? Yet I know
You cannot live on someone else's terms.
Nonetheless I go on loving
and these tears,
this broken heart,
is the price I pray for love.
The love we shared was well worth it,
and I would do it again...
but I wonder if I ever will.

About the Poet

Anthony Signorelli, also known as The Sailing Poet, is a co-editor of *Inroads: Men · Creativity · Soul* and served previously as the poetry editor for Holy Cow! Press. He co-edited the anthology Rooster Crows at Light from the Bombing and in addition has published six non-fiction books, including:

- *Call to Liberty: Bridging the Divide Between Liberals and Conservatives*, 2006

- *Speculations on Postcapitalism*, 2017

- *What Is Liberalism?* 2018

- *The Great Mechanism: The Power Behind the Relentless Juggernaut of Western Capitalism*, 2018

- *Consent Is Not Enough: What Men Need to Know in an #MeToo World*, 2021

- *What Is Postcapitalism? Imagining the World After Capitalism and Socialism*, 2025

Anthony organizes a monthly open mic in his small home town in northern Wisconsin, where he shares these and other poems regularly. His current work explores grief, climate change, the AI revolution, and the eloquence of the heart. You can find it at anthonysignorelli.substack.com.

9 798995 340607